Sara L
Teen Detective

Lesley Thompson

Founder Editors: Bill Bowler and Sue Parminter

Illustrated by Amit Tayal

Lesley Thompson was born in the North of England, but now lives near Alicante in Spain. She loves reading, the cinema, music, laughing with her friends, and looking at the sea. She also enjoys walking in the countryside in England and Spain, and one day she hopes to walk the Camino de Santiago in northern Spain. Lesley has also written *Lisa's Song*, *Deep Trouble*, *The Real McCoy and Other Ghost Stories*, *Zombie Attack!*, and *V is for Vampire*.

OXFORD
UNIVERSITY PRESS

OXFORD
UNIVERSITY PRESS

Great Clarendon Street, Oxford, OX2 6DP,
United Kingdom

Oxford University Press is a department of the University
of Oxford. It furthers the University's objective of excellence
in research, scholarship, and education by publishing
worldwide. Oxford is a registered trade mark of Oxford
University Press in the UK and in certain other countries

ISBN: 978 0 19 424573 9   Book
ISBN: 978 0 19 462248 6   Book and Audio Pack

Audio not available separately

Printed in China

This book is printed on paper from certified and
well-managed sources.

ACKNOWLEDGEMENTS

Cover image and illustrations by: Amit Tayal

*The publisher would like to thank the following for their permission to
reproduce photographs*: Alamy Stock Photo; pp.24 (Paris street/
vulnificans), 57 (vintage book/Richard Levine), Getty Images;
pp.56 (John Grisham/Patrick McMullan).

Contents

BEFORE READING

1 Match the pictures with the description of the people. Use a dictionary to help you.

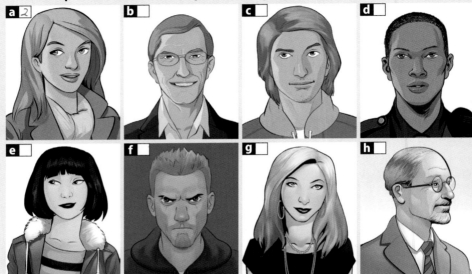

1 Cody, a violent criminal.
2 Sara Dixon, a student who likes detective work.
3 Mr. Grainger, a teacher at Sara's school.
4 Sandy, a young policeman.

5 Luke, Sara's boyfriend.
6 Carlie, Sara's best friend.
7 Mr. Dixon, Sara's father.
8 Gina, a rich new student.

2 What do you think happens in *Sara Dixon, Teen Detective*? Complete the sentences with the names from Activity 1.

a .... doesn't know that his daughter Sara is investigating a crime.

b Sara's friend .... knows Luke and she likes him.

c .... is older than his girlfriend Sara and he has a small company.

d .... is trying to get money from Sara and he threatens her.

e .... has money but she tries to get more from Cody.

f .... knows that Sara is a good student but he is worried about her exams.

g .... tells Sara to leave the investigation to the police.

h .... has helped the police before but this time she is in danger.

Compare your answers with a partner.

CHAPTER ONE
THE ACCIDENT

At nine o'clock on Saturday morning, Sara Dixon looked out of the window of her bedroom. The sky was gray and it was raining a little. Sara was getting ready to go out. She was happy that today was not a school day. This was her last year and the work was getting harder all the time. She had to do well in the coming **exams**. But just for today, she wasn't studying – she had other plans.

Sara's father looked through the door of her room. He was wearing his coat. Mr. Dixon lived alone with Sara, his only child. He worked for the police in a **laboratory** and he loved his job. His daughter enjoyed listening to all his interesting stories and one day she wanted to work for the police too. She planned to go to **university** next year, but first she had to do those difficult exams.

'Are you going out today, Sara?' Mr. Dixon asked.

'Yes, Dad,' she said. 'Luke's coming for me and we're going to the **mall**. We'll have something to eat there, I think.'

'OK, then,' he said. 'I'll see you later. I have to do some work at the lab. Have a good time.'

exam a student takes these to see how much he or she knows

laboratory/lab a room where a scientist works

university people study here after they leave school

mall a building with a lot of different stores and places to eat

1

Luke was Sara's boyfriend. They usually met at the weekends because they were both busy during the week. Luke left school last year and he was trying to start an **IT company**. A lot of people wanted to do the same thing and Luke wasn't finding life easy. Sara hoped that he was in a good **mood** today. He was very quiet these days and it was sometimes hard to talk to him.

The doorbell rang and Sara went to answer it. Luke was standing outside. She smiled at him, but he did not smile back. 'He's in a bad mood again,' Sara thought darkly.

The mall was very bright, and busy with crowds of Saturday shoppers. Sara and Luke walked past the many stores, coffee bars and places to eat. Once or twice, Luke looked **nervously** behind him.

IT company a business that works with Information Technology or computers

mood when you are in a good mood, you feel happy

nervous a little afraid or worried

'What is it, Luke? Have you seen someone that you know?' Sara asked.

'No, I haven't,' he replied.

Suddenly, Luke stopped in front of a store which sold jeans and he **stared** into the window. Sara looked too and she saw that her boyfriend wasn't looking at the clothes. He was staring at something behind him which was **reflected** in the glass. She looked too and saw a thin, dark man standing a few meters behind them. Was he following them?

'Do you know him?' Sara said to Luke.

'Who?' asked Luke. 'What are you talking about? I'm looking at the jeans.'

stare to look at something or someone for a long time

reflect to show a picture of something, e.g. in the glass of a window

The man turned and walked away. Suddenly, Luke wasn't interested in the jeans any longer, and he looked at Sara. He tried to smile.

'Let's have something to eat,' he said.

'All right. Where shall we go?' asked Sara brightly.

'Anywhere,' said Luke shortly. 'I'm not all that hungry.'

'Is anything the matter?' asked Sara. 'You look worried.'

'No, I'm fine. Look, here's a place that sells sandwiches. Let's go there.'

They sat down and waited without speaking for their food to arrive. Sara tried again to start a conversation. When she spoke, Luke jumped a little.

'How are things at work?' she asked.

Luke stared down at the table. He answered without looking up at Sara.

'OK, I **guess**. We need to buy some new computers but it isn't a good time right now. We'll have to wait a few months,' he said.

'Oh well,' she answered, smiling. 'You're very good at your job. I'm sure things will get better.'

'How can you know that, Sara?' asked Luke suddenly. He sounded nervous and angry. 'You're always so happy!'

'You always liked that about me before,' said Sara. 'I'm only trying to help.'

'I know. I'm sorry,' said Luke. 'But you sometimes forget that we don't all have money like you. Life isn't always easy.'

Sara looked at her boyfriend in surprise. It was true that she and her father did not have money troubles. Her mother was from a rich family. But two years ago she died very suddenly, and since then Sara and her dad often felt unhappy and alone. Luke knew this, so he never usually spoke to her in this way. Was he really just worried about work or was there something more? He often became angry with her these days. Was he bored with her?

They finished their food in uncomfortable **silence**. Without looking in any more stores, they left the mall and walked out

guess to think something when you are not very sure

silence when a person doesn't speak

into the street. It was very busy with lots of traffic and crowds of shoppers. The lights were on green for the traffic and they waited to cross the street. Suddenly, there was a loud noise of car **brakes** and a cry went up from the **sidewalk** opposite them.

Somebody was lying in the street. People were screaming and shouting. Sara began to move quickly **towards** the **scene** of the accident.

'Come on, Luke!' she shouted. 'Perhaps we can help!'

But Luke was pulling her back by her arm. His face was white and he was staring at something in the crowd opposite.

'No! We can't do anything. Look, I have to go. I've just remembered something. It's about work and it's important. I'll call you later,' he said quickly. 'Bye.'

Before Sara could say anything, Luke left her and he was running away through the crowds.

Sara looked after him for a minute. He usually wanted to help people. What was wrong with him? But he was moving quickly and soon she could not see him anymore. Sara crossed the street and walked towards the circle of people who were standing around something on the ground.

brakes (*verb to* **brake**) the things on a car which help you to stop or go more slowly

sidewalk this is where people walk, at the side of the street

towards going to

scene the place where something happens

READING CHECK

1 Are these sentences true or false? Tick the boxes.

		True	False
a	Sara's mom dies before the story begins	☑	☐
b	Mr. Dixon works for the police.	☐	☐
c	Luke is a student at Sara's school.	☐	☐
d	Luke and Sara go to the mall.	☐	☐
e	Luke is in a very good mood.	☐	☐
f	Luke sees something in the mall that makes him nervous.	☐	☐
g	Luke helps Sara after the accident.	☐	☐

2 Match the first and second parts of the sentence.

a 'Are you going out?'   **1** Sara asks herself.

b 'Is there something wrong with him?'   **2** Luke asks Sara.

c 'I'm not very hungry.'   **3** Luke says quickly.

d 'You're good at your job.'   **4** Mr. Dixon asks Sara.

e 'Why are you always so happy?'   **5** Luke tells Sara.

f 'I have to go!'   **6** Sara says to Luke.

WORD WORK

Use suitable forms of the words in the traffic lights to complete the sentences on the next page.

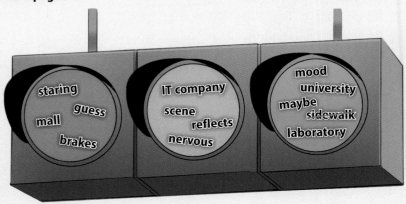

staring   guess   mall   brakes

IT company   scene   reflects   nervous

mood   university   maybe   sidewalk   laboratory

a The ..*sidewalk*.. is for people, not traffic.

b I'm not sure, but I think that . . . . he's afraid of her.

c He's in a bad . . . . because he's lost his job.

d The . . . . on this car are very good. The car stops in seconds!

e That man is . . . . at me again. Do I have food on my face?

f When he finishes school my son is going to . . . . to study languages.

g Her parents have a small . . . . and she works there. She's very good with computers.

h My hands are shaking. I'm always . . . . when I meet new people.

i I want to buy something for John's birthday. Let's go to the . . . .

j I love it when the water . . . . the evening light.

k I'll go to the party, I . . . . , but I don't really want to go.

l After the accident, the . . . . in the street was terrible. Everyone was crying.

m I would like to work in a . . . . , but I'm not good at science.

GUESS WHAT

Which of these things do you think happen in the next chapter? Tick four boxes.

a ☐ Luke dies in the accident.

b ☐ Sara goes to look at the accident.

c ☐ The police and ambulance arrive.

d ☐ Sara goes to the hospital in the ambulance.

e ☐ Sandy arrives and talks to Sara.

f ☐ Sara tells Sandy that she knows the person in the accident.

g ☐ Sara runs away from Sandy.

h ☐ Sandy and Sara go to Sara's school.

CHAPTER TWO
THE STUDENT

Sara came nearer to the group of people. She looked down and saw a girl lying on the ground. The girl's body was strangely **twisted** and there was a look of **shock** on her face. There was blood near her mouth and under her head. A woman standing near the girl was crying quietly.

'The poor girl,' she said to Sara. 'I don't know what happened to her. She was in front of me and then she suddenly fell over into the street. The car couldn't stop in time and it knocked her down.'

The driver of the car, an old man, was crying with his hands over his face. His wife was holding him and shaking from shock.

Sara looked again at the body on the ground. Slowly her face changed and she put her hands to her mouth. She **recognized** that girl! It was **Gina** Lowfield and she was a student at Sara's school. Sara did not know her well because Gina was a **boarder** and a new girl at the school.

twisted not straight

shock a feeling of surprise at something very bad

recognize to see someone and to know who it is

Gina /ˈdʒinə/

boarder a student who lives and sleeps at a school

Police cars and ambulances were arriving at the scene. Sara recognized Sandy, a young policeman who was a friend of her father's. He saw Sara in the crowd and ran up to her. 'What happened, Sara? Did you see the accident?' asked Sandy.

'Not really,' she replied. 'I was on the other sidewalk and I heard a lot of noise and shouting. Then there was the sound of brakes. It was very loud.'

'So there was noise and shouting before the car braked?' asked Sandy.

'Well, there was noise before and after, I guess,' answered Sara. 'Anyway, the next minute, Gina was lying in the street.'

'Gina?' said Sandy, surprised. 'Do you know her?'

'I know who she is,' Sara replied. 'Her name is Gina Lowfield and she's a boarder at my school. She hasn't been there long. I don't know much about her. Is she going to be all right?'

'I don't know,' answered Sandy. 'She hit her head very hard on the ground, I think. The **medic** is looking at her now in the ambulance.'

The people in the crowd were standing around quietly now. **medic** a doctor

They were waiting to hear the news from inside the ambulance. After twenty minutes, the medic climbed down and walked up to Sandy. 'There's nothing more that we can do,' he began. He tried to speak quietly in Sandy's ear, but Sara could hear some of his words, too. 'I'm afraid she's dead. The poor girl hit her head very badly on the street, and she had a number of other **injuries**,' he said. 'But I still don't understand how it all happened.'

'I think it was just a terrible accident,' said Sandy. 'The lights were on green for the traffic, so I don't think she was trying to cross the street. I guess that with all the crowds she **tripped** and fell into the street. The poor driver just couldn't stop in time.'

The medic left Sandy and Sara and went back to the ambulance. Sara stood silently, with her head down. She felt terrible about Gina's death, but she was also remembering Luke's strange **reaction** to the accident. After a minute, Sandy spoke. 'Look, Sara, you can't do anything for poor Gina here. You say that she was a boarder at your school. Why don't you come with us to her room? Perhaps you can help us with our questions.'

'All right,' agreed Sara. She usually enjoyed helping with police **investigations**, but she felt that this was a little different.

) NOT CROSS   CRIME SCENE - DO NOT CROSS   CRIME SCENE - DO NOT CROSS

Gina's room at the school was small and very untidy. There were clothes on the bed and over the chair. On the desk, there was an expensive computer. There were also some beautiful pieces of gold **jewelry**.

'Look at this! That's surprising, isn't it?' said Sandy. 'Students don't usually have nice jewelry like that in their room.'

'Perhaps not, but you need money if you want to be a boarder at our school,' said Sara. Sara was only a day girl but her dad paid a lot of money to send her to the school.

Sandy quickly looked around the room again. 'I'll come back here later,' he said. 'First, I'll have to speak to the teachers. We

injury someone who is hurt in an accident can have injuries to their body

trip to hit your foot against something and fall

reaction the way you speak and what you do after something happens

investigation something that a policeman or detective does to understand how or why a crime has happened

jewelry expensive things that people wear like gold rings

need the phone number of Gina's family. I hope that I don't have to make that call. It will be very difficult.'

Sara said goodbye to Sandy and walked slowly out into the street. Her legs were shaking. She was beginning to have a reaction to Gina's sudden death. Just then, she really wanted to talk to Luke. She needed to hear the sound of his voice and to know that everything was all right between them. Quickly, she took her phone from the pocket of her jeans and called him.

To Sara's surprise the phone went straight to **voice mail**. She waited. 'Perhaps he'll call back when he sees that it's me,' she thought. But minutes went by and there was no call. Why wasn't Luke answering? Where was he and what was he doing?

voice mail when a person doesn't answer a phone call, you can leave a message on this

READING CHECK

Correct the mistakes in these sentences.

a Sara sees a ~~boy~~ lying on the ground. *girl*

b The driver of the car is an old woman.

c Gina is a teacher at Sara's school

d Gina dies a long time after the accident

e The traffic lights were on red when Gina fell into the street.

f Gina's room at the school is very tidy.

g There is a television on her desk.

h You can't go to Gina and Sara's school if you are rich.

i After she leaves Gina's room, Sara feels very happy.

j Sara can't talk to Luke because he isn't answering his door.

WORD WORK

Choose the best word to complete each sentence.

a It was dark in the room and he *tripped* / *twisted* and fell down.

b The little girl is a *medic* / *boarder* at the school, but she comes home at the weekend.

c After the accident, his leg was all *twisted* / *tripped*.

d He can't play football because the *injury* / *reaction* to his arm is still bad.

e She had a bad *injury* / *reaction* to the death of her dog and she cried all night.

f Her husband doesn't have the money to buy expensive *jewelry* / *investigation*.

g It was a terrible *trip* / *shock* when the train crashed.

h This is bad – call a *medic* / *injury*!

i The police *reaction* / *investigation* showed that the man died by accident.

j I didn't *recognize* / *trip* him at first after all these years.

GUESS WHAT

Which of these things do you think happens in the next chapter? Write *Yes* or *No*.

a Sara tries to phone Luke again.

....

b Sara goes to Luke's apartment.

....

c Luke hides inside his apartment.

....

d Mr. Dixon tells Sara that Luke is bad.

....

e Sara goes to the river and finds Luke's jacket. ....

f Sara finds Luke's phone.

....

CHAPTER THREE
THE BOATHOUSE

Luke lived in a small **apartment** with his older brother, Dan, not far from the center of town. Dan worked long hours, and he was often out at his office. Sara decided to go and **confront** Luke. 'He must tell me what's wrong,' she said to herself. 'I can't go on like this.' On the way, she tried to call Luke again but there was no reply.

Outside in the street, she **buzzed** the number of Luke's apartment and waited. There was no answer. She thought that perhaps he was hiding in there, hiding from her. Suddenly Sara felt very angry. She pushed open the door to the building, walked inside, and went up to the fifth floor. There was a key to Luke's apartment in her pocket. They agreed that it was 'only for important times'. Well, this was important to her! 'I hope that you're not hiding in there, Luke,' she said to herself as she knocked on the door of apartment 5C. Once more, there was only silence. 'OK, Luke, this has gone too far,' said Sara. She put the key in the lock and pushed open the door.

There was no sound of a TV or a radio – just deep silence. The apartment had a living room, two bedrooms and a bathroom. Sara quickly found out that they were all empty. She sat down near the window and stared out into the street. People were hurrying up and down the sidewalk. She stayed like that for some time. When her phone suddenly buzzed and broke the silence, she sat up. There was a **text message** for her. Was it finally Luke? She stared at the words on the phone. Slowly she understood what they meant.

apartment
a number of rooms in a building where someone lives

confront
to try and find out the truth about something from someone

buzz to make a hard, ringing sound

text message
you write this on your phone when you want to tell someone something

> If you want to see your boyfriend alive, come to the river near Clark's boathouse at midnight. Come alone and don't tell anyone.

Sara looked at her phone. It was from Luke's number. What did it all mean? Was it real? Was he playing with her? Or was there another **reason**? Sara was beginning to worry. She left the apartment and locked the door. She decided to go to the boathouse that night, but she wanted to go alone. If Luke was playing with her, she didn't want to look stupid in front of the police.

Sara waited at home that evening. She talked with her father about Gina and then they watched TV together. Gina's death was on the news. The news reader described her death as 'a terrible accident.' Sara decided to say nothing to her father about the text message.

She was beginning to think that there was something badly wrong with Luke. Now she was feeling more angry than worried. She had to confront Luke alone and find out what the trouble was.

After Mr. Dixon went to bed at eleven o'clock, Sara climbed the stairs to her room. She put on some warmer clothes and took a **flashlight** from her cupboard. Quietly, she left the house and began to walk down towards the river. It was about twenty minutes to the meeting place on foot. At first, she went past small groups of people enjoying their Saturday night, but she soon left the busy streets behind.

reason why you do something

flashlight a small light that you carry in your hand

Sara hurried onto the **path** along by the river. It was dark and quiet with tall trees on one side. She then walked under the old bridge and just before midnight, she arrived at the small boathouse. She waited outside and, now and again, she **shone** her flashlight into the dark night around her. The only sounds came from the water in the river and from small animals moving around in the grass. The time went by and Sara waited nervously. Nobody came. Every two or three minutes she looked at her phone but there was no message.

Finally, at 12.15, she pushed open the door of the boathouse. It was dark inside, but by the light of her flashlight she could see into every corner of the small building. Her eyes fell on an old, **upturned** boat. There was something lying on top of it. Sara looked more carefully. It was a dark blue coat. She picked it up and recognized it at once. 'This is Luke's coat!' she thought.

path a narrow street for people to walk along

shine (*past* **shone**) to put the light of a flashlight on something

upturned with the top of something at the bottom

With horror, she saw that there was something dark on the front – it was blood, and it was still wet.

'This isn't funny, Luke,' Sara said to herself. She went outside again and stared into the dark night. Nothing moved and there was only the sound of the river running past. Sara was beginning to feel cold. She moved a few meters towards the river and looked out over the water.

'Luke? Are you there? Luke?' Sara said. Her voice sounded small and shaky. There was no answer. 'Come out, Luke!' Sara was shouting now and she was shaking with anger. Only silence met her words.

She waited ten minutes more and then finally decided to leave. Nobody was coming that night. She held Luke's coat to her body and hurried back along the dark path by the river. She felt more worried than ever.

READING CHECK

Put these sentences in the correct order. Number them 1–10.

a ☐ Sara finds a jacket.

b ☐ Sara visits Luke's apartment.

c ☐ Mr. Dixon goes to bed at eleven o'clock.

d ☐ Sara puts on some warmer clothes.

e ☐ She goes home and watches TV with her dad.

f ☐ She gets a message on her phone.

g ☐ She walks to the river.

h ☐ She sees that the jacket has blood on it.

i ☐ She goes inside the boathouse.

j ☐ She looks down at the pavement from Luke's window.

WORD WORK

1 Find words or phrases from Chapter 3 in the boats.

a ...reason...　　b ....　　c ....

d ....　　e ....　　f ....

g ....　　h ....　　i ....

2 Complete the sentences with the words from Activity 1.

a When someone calls me, my phone gives a very loud ..... _buzz_ ....

b After the fight, there were .... chairs and tables all over the room.

c I must .... my girlfriend and ask her if she took my money.

d Why did he do it? I don't know the ....

e Take the .... next to the river and walk until you see some houses.

f I like to see the sun .... It makes me feel happy.

g There's a .... on my phone from my friend in Australia.

h There are no lights in here and I can't see. I need a ....

i He has a big .... in the city center.

GUESS WHAT

Who do you think says these things in the next chapter? Write _Carlie_ or _Sara_.

a I wanted to ask about Luke. ....

b Yesterday he left me in the street. ....

c That poor girl. Did you see what happened? ....

d What happened last night? ....

e Have you seen Luke today? ....

f Luke told me that he needs money. ....

CHAPTER FOUR
CARLIE

Sara looked behind her. Were those **footsteps** that she could hear? She began to walk more quickly. Finally, she started to run. She did not stop until she saw the bright lights of the store windows. It was late and the streets were almost empty. She thought about her friend Carlie and how she never went to bed before two o'clock in the morning. She had to phone her. She really needed to talk to someone.

At last, she arrived home. She did not want to wake up her father, so she went into the kitchen and quietly closed the door behind her. She called Carlie and she was very happy when her friend answered after the third ring.

footsteps the noise people make with their feet when they walk

'Hey, Sara. What are you doing up so late? This isn't like you!' she laughed.

'Hi Carlie. I just needed to talk,' said Sara. 'You weren't asleep, were you?'

'Of course not!' replied Carlie. 'You know me, Sara. I come alive at night. How are things?'

'Er, not too good. Can we meet somewhere in the morning?' said Sara. 'I need to ask you something. I can't talk now because Dad's in bed and I don't want to wake him up.'

Carlie did not answer immediately. To Sara's surprise, her friend sounded strangely nervous.

'Er, yes, sure. I'll meet you in Joe's coffee bar. Is ten o'clock all right?' she asked.

'Yes, that's great,' answered Sara. 'I'll explain then. I'll see you tomorrow, Carlie. Bye.'

Sara felt less nervous. She always felt better after talking to her friend. Carlie knew Luke and her dad well too, so she understood everything about Sara's life.

NOT CROSS   CRIME SCENE - DO NOT CROSS   CRIME SCENE-DO NOT CROSS

The next morning, the girls met in the coffee bar. Sara was **pale** and tired. She didn't sleep well. And now that she was with her friend, she did not feel so happy. Carlie looked uncomfortable. She talked looking down at her cup and did not meet Sara's eyes.

'So what's the problem, Sara?' asked Carlie.

'I wanted to know about Luke, really,' said Sara. 'Is it just me, or has he been a little strange lately?'

There was silence for a few seconds. Carlie drank some of her coffee before answering.

'Luke? Strange? No. Why do you ask?' she said.

'Well, he's always in a bad mood,' replied Sara 'He's so nervous and he gets angry for no reason. Yesterday, he suddenly left me in the street. There was an accident and he just walked away.'

pale without a lot of color

'Oh, yes, that poor girl who died,' said Carlie 'Did you see what happened?'

'Yes, Luke and I were on the other side of the street,' began Sara. 'But the strange thing is that Luke didn't want to help. It wasn't like him. He just ran away. I can't understand it. Then last night...' Sara stopped. For some reason, she did not want to tell Carlie about the boathouse.

'What happened last night?' asked Carlie, interested.

'Oh, nothing important,' she replied. 'I don't want to talk about it. I'm just worried about Luke, that's all.'

Carlie looked at Sara and she spoke carefully.

'You know that Luke is having problems with his company, don't you?' she said.

'Yes, but he won't talk about them,' answered Sara. 'Has he said anything to you?' Suddenly, she felt **suspicious**.

'He told me that he needs money and he doesn't know where to get it,' said Carlie. 'Someone is helping him, I think. But I'm not sure.'

'Who?' asked Sara quickly. 'Do you know them?'

'No, no. I'm only guessing,' said Carlie. 'He hasn't said much to me really.' Carlie looked up, but she couldn't meet Sara's eyes.

A terrible **suspicion** came into Sara's head. Carlie knew something and she wasn't telling her. Her friend was spending a lot of time with Luke. What if they were more than friends?

'Carlie,' said Sara, 'Have you spoken to Luke today?'

suspicious
when you feel that something is not right

suspicion the feeling that something is not right

'No, I haven't,' said Carlie. 'I really don't know anything else. Don't worry about Luke. He'll be OK. He'll tell you everything sooner or later.'

'What do you mean by "everything"?' asked Sara.

'I don't mean anything by it! You're not thinking straight,' replied Carlie. 'Look, I need to go. I'll see you on Monday, OK? Try not to worry.'

Carlie said goodbye and left quickly. By the time she was at the door of the coffee bar, she was nearly running.

Sara sat still for a while, thinking. Her best friend and her boyfriend were being very strange. How could she study for her exams with all these things happening to her?

Sara tried to read a school book at home that afternoon but she just couldn't study. She thought again and again about Luke and Carlie. Just after four o'clock, her phone buzzed and she looked at it quickly. It was another text message:

> You've seen the coat and now you know that I'm **serious**. Last night was just a **test**. Tomorrow night is the real thing. Come to the same place at the same time and bring $50,000 in **cash**. Do NOT tell the police or something terrible will happen. I know that your dad has money, and I know all about you. Do NOT do anything stupid!

Once more, the message was from Luke's phone. But Sara wasn't at all sure that the message was from Luke. It didn't sound like him. Her head buzzed with questions.

'Why doesn't he just ask me for money if he needs it?' she said to herself. 'Someone is trying to **blackmail** me, but who is it? And is Luke in danger or is he really trying to get money from me to help his company?'

In the end, Sara had one important question that she couldn't forget. Luke knew Sara and her dad well. But how well did they really know Luke?

serious not joking or playing

test when you do something to a person to see what they do

cash paper money and coins

blackmail to get money from someone by saying that you will do bad things if they don't pay you

23

READING CHECK

Match the first and second parts of the sentences.

a Sara phones Carlie

b The girls meet the next day

c Carlie is uncomfortable

d Sara doesn't tell Carlie

e Carlie knows that Luke

f Sara gets a text message

g Sara can't believe

1 that Luke has sent the message.

2 is having trouble with his company.

3 asking for money.

4 about the boathouse.

5 at a coffee bar.

6 with Sara.

7 because she wants to talk to her.

WORD WORK

1 **Find six more words from Chapter 4 in the letter square.**

P	S	U	S	P	I	C	I	O	U	S
I	A	B	T	E	S	T	K	T	S	M
Q	U	L	E	A	U	D	G	Z	E	U
K	W	E	E	M	R	B	H	F	R	C
F	O	O	T	S	T	E	P	S	I	E
C	P	A	O	S	W	H	J	E	O	R
A	Y	K	B	F	C	X	B	Q	U	B
S	V	T	J	I	T	O	M	S	S	I
H	X	H	R	T	E	B	R	K	P	P
B	L	A	C	K	M	A	I	L	O	T

2 **Complete the sentences with the correct form of the words in Activity 1.**

a You're very . . . . Are you feeling all right?

b I don't know… let's do a . . . .

c She knows something bad about his past and she is . . . . him.

d I can hear . . . . behind us. Is someone following us?

e Why are you so . . . . ? I haven't done anything wrong!

f You have to pay in . . . . in this store. They don't take anything else.

GUESS WHAT

What do you think happens in the next chapter? Write _Yes_ or _No_.

a There is something on TV about Gina's death. . . . .

b Sara decides to forget about Gina's death. . . . .

c A student tells Sara about a party in Gina's room. . . . .

d Sara finds Luke in Gina's room. . . . .

CHAPTER FIVE
GINA'S SECRET

Sara slept badly again that night. Early on Monday morning, she watched the news on TV before leaving for school. The first news story was about Gina. A man was **reporting** on the police investigation from the scene of the accident.

'Police are still trying to understand the death of seventeen-year-old student Gina Lowfield. Gina fell in front of a car here on Saturday morning and died soon after. At first, police spoke of an accident, but now they have some important questions about her death. There were a lot of people on the sidewalk at the time. Gina tripped and fell into the street, they said. However, some **witnesses** now say that someone pushed Gina and that a man ran away from the scene.

'The police have spoken to students from Gina's class. They said that she was a quiet girl and did not have many friends because she was new to the school. The police also want to know why the student had expensive jewelry and a lot of cash in her room. Any witnesses to the accident, or people who knew Gina well, need to speak to the police immediately.'

Sara remembered Luke's shock at the accident and how he ran away from the scene.

Was there a **connection** between Luke and Gina? At school, she decided to forget about the first class of the day and visit Gina's room again.

report to tell or write about something that has happened

witness a person who sees something important and can say later that it happened

connection something that puts people or things together

tape a long, thin piece of paper

Mara /ˈmɑrə/

⟩ NOT CROSS   CRIME SCENE - DO NOT CROSS   CRIME SCENE - DO NOT CROSS

When she arrived, there was a yellow police **tape** across the door with the words CRIME SCENE, DO NOT CROSS. While she was standing there, she saw **Mara** Connors, another student at the school. She recognized Sara and came up to her.

'Poor Gina. I know that she wasn't very friendly, but what a terrible thing to happen,' she said.

'Yes, terrible,' agreed Sara. 'I didn't know her very well. Did you know her?'

'A little. She seemed happy at the school. Of course, she was unlucky with the **robbery** and everything.'

'What robbery?' asked Sara in surprise.

'About a week ago, someone went into her

room and took her phone and some of her things,' explained Mara. 'She was very unhappy at first but then she told me that everything was OK and she wasn't worried any more. Perhaps the thief was another student and they gave her the things back.'

'Did she tell the police about the robbery?' asked Sara.

'I think so, but I don't know, really,' said Mara. 'As I said before, she looked happier so I didn't talk about it with her.'

'Right,' Sara said. 'That's all very interesting.'

Sara walked outside the building into the gardens. It was quiet there and the only sounds came from the singing of the birds. She sat down on one of the seats under the tall old trees and took out her phone.

'Hi, Sandy. Can you do something for me?' she asked. 'Find out if Gina Lowfield reported a robbery in her room about ten days ago.'

'A robbery? That's news to me. OK, Sara. I'm looking at the computer now. Give me a minute,' he said. 'No, there's nothing here about a robbery. Why are you asking?'

robbery when a thief takes things from someone or somewhere

'Oh, it's nothing important,' said Sara. 'Thanks for your time, Sandy.'

'But listen,' said Sandy, 'If you know something new about Gina, you must tell the police. Don't do any investigations by yourself.'

'I won't,' replied Sara. 'It's nothing serious. Thanks for your help.'

Sara finished the call before Sandy could ask her anything more.

'This is important,' thought Sara. 'Why didn't Gina report the robbery? For some reason, Gina didn't want to talk to the police. Perhaps she had something to hide. Perhaps there was a connection between the robbery and her death. If there is a connection, I need to look at her computer. That means going into her room and I don't have a key. Oh well, it isn't the first time I've done this.' She felt inside her pocket and took out a small **hairpin**.

Sara went back into the building and walked up to Gina's door. The building was quieter now. Most people were in class. She had to do something and she had to do it now. She looked to the right and left. There was nobody near. Quickly, she took down the yellow police tape.

'Hello again,' a voice said suddenly in her ear. It was Mara. She was standing next to another student, a tall, pale girl with long hair. The two girls were holding some yellow and white flowers in their hands.

'We wanted to leave some flowers outside Gina's room,' began Mara, but then she stopped. 'Why have you taken down the police tape?' she asked.

hairpin a thin thing that you use to keep your hair in place

29

Sara thought quickly. 'It was an accident. I wanted to leave a note on her door saying that I was sorry and the tape fell off,' she explained. 'But you're right, you know, flowers are much better than a note. I'll go and buy some now. See you later. Bye!'

She walked away, leaving the two girls staring after her. They left their flowers on the floor next to Gina's room and went back to class. Sara waited round the corner for a few minutes, then she went back quickly. She tried to open Gina's door but it was locked. She took the hairpin from her pocket and put it into the lock. It made a small sound. She pushed the door open easily and went into the room.

Quietly, she closed the door behind her. There was very little time before classes ended.

'If the police find me here, they'll think that I have something to do with Gina's death and perhaps with Luke's **disappearance**,' she thought. 'I must be quick.'

disappearance
when a person goes away and nobody can find them

READING CHECK

Correct nine more mistakes in the story.

badly

Sara sleeps very ~~well~~ that night. She watches the news on TV and learns more about Gina. She

decides to go to Luke's room. When she is there, she meets a girl called Mara, a teacher at the

school. She tells Sara that something happened to Gina a few days before. Someone went

into her room and broke some of her things. Sara decides to call Mr. Dixon. She goes into the

classroom and makes the call. When she goes back to Gina's room, Mara is there again with a

boy. They are carrying some books and they want to leave them inside Gina's room. They are

suspicious of Sara and she has to go away again. She hides around the corner and waits. She

goes back to Gina's room and opens the window. She knows that she hasn't got much time.

WORD WORK

1 Complete the crossword with six words from Chapter 5.

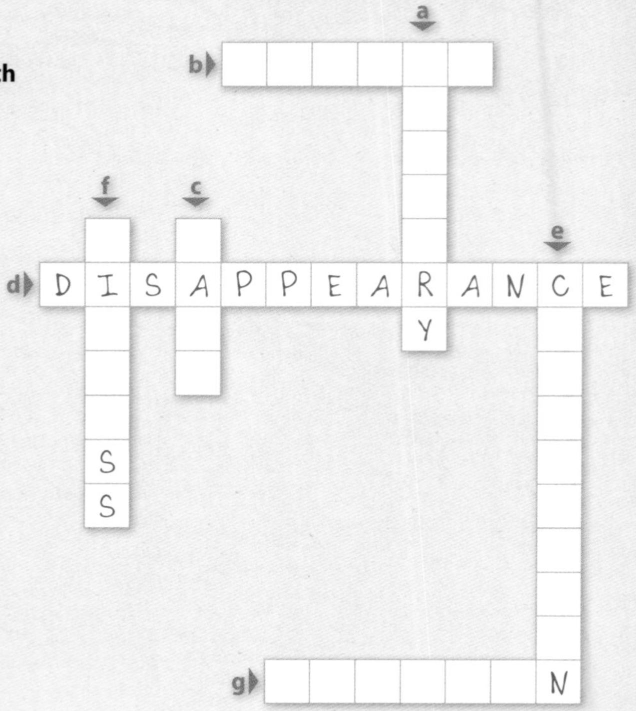

d▶ D I S A P P E A R A N C E

S
S

Y

g▶ N

2 Use the words in Activity 1 to complete the sentences.

a The boy's . . . . worried his parents terribly.

b The . . . . heard a shout, but didn't see anything.

c That police . . . . across the door means that we can't go inside.

d There is no . . . . between that man and the murder. He was out of the country at the time.

e There was a . . . . at my bank last week. They took thousands of dollars.

f Your hair is falling down again. I'll put a . . . . in it.

g There's a . . . . on TV about it.

GUESS WHAT

What do you think happens in the next chapter? Complete the sentences with the people's names.

a . . . . finds something interesting on Gina's computer.

b . . . . notices that Sara is worried about something.

c Sara and . . . . have supper together.

d Sara goes to the boathouse where . . . . is waiting.

e . . . . is in the boathouse and he is hurt.

f Sara phones . . . . and asks for help.

CHAPTER SIX
LUKE IS IN DANGER

Gina's expensive new computer was still on the desk. Sara opened it and looked quickly through the **files**. She soon found what she was looking for. There were some interesting email messages from Gina to an unnamed person asking for money. The latest one said, 'Send me the money soon. If not, I'll go to the police and tell them all about you.'

'So, she was blackmailing this person,' thought Sara.

There were also a number of photos. Someone took them on Gina's stolen phone a few days ago and they came up on Gina's computer. One of the pictures showed a thin, dark man who was smiling stupidly into the camera. 'I think I recognize you,' said Sara quietly. 'It wasn't very clever to take a photo of yourself on Gina's phone, was it?' The connection between Gina's death and the robbery was starting to come out. But what was the connection with Luke's disappearance?

file a place on a computer where you can keep information

Sara closed the computer and left the room quietly. She put the police tape across the door and tried to walk away slowly.

Sara had to decide about visiting the boathouse again. Perhaps Luke was playing with her. But surely he wasn't asking for $50,000 in blackmail money? So who was doing this? Luke was in real danger, she thought. She had to try to help him. So she began to make plans for the evening.

School that day was difficult for Sara. She couldn't study at all. She was thinking about her plans and everything she needed to do.

Towards the end of the lesson, her favorite teacher, Mr. Grainger, looked at her. 'Sara Dixon,' he said. 'You really need to work harder if you're going to do well in your exams.'

'What? Oh, yes, sorry, I'm a little tired today,' said Sara.

Mr. Grainger smiled at her. Sara was a good student and he wasn't really worried about her studies. And, of course, he thought sadly, all the students were unhappy and worried because of Gina's death.

That evening, Sara got ready to go to the boathouse again. She

looked in the cupboard and found a large, strong bag which she **filled** with old newspapers. It didn't look much like $50,000 but it was the best she could do.

She looked through her clothes and took out an old coat with big pockets. In one pocket, she put her flashlight and phone. In the other pocket, she put something from her father's cupboard – a **taser** which he had for his work. With this, she could fight off anyone. 'Sorry, Dad,' she said to herself. 'I know you're going to be angry when you find out about this. But I couldn't tell you or the police about Luke. His life is in serious danger right now and I must do everything to help him.'

Now she had to wait. Again and again, she looked at her watch. The hands moved round very slowly. Sara and her father had supper together in front of the television. Mr. Dixon was tired and he went to bed early. Sara watched the late night news by herself. There was nothing more about Gina's death.

fill to make something full

taser an electric gun that stops people moving or running away

At 11.30, she took the large bag from her room and then put on her coat. She left the dark house quietly and started to walk down to the river. The streets were quieter than on Saturday. A man standing on a corner stared at her and she began to feel afraid. She went on to the narrow path by the river. It was raining a little and the path was wet.

When she walked under the old bridge, her footsteps sounded loud. Soon, she saw the boathouse again, and she stopped suddenly. It looked dark and lonely. But was it empty? She walked slowly up to the small building and began to put her hand out. But before she could touch the door, it flew open and someone pulled her inside. She tripped over and dropped the bag on the floor.

'Hey, what are you doing?' she shouted.

'Sit down and shut your mouth,' a man's hard voice said loudly. 'Sit over there on the boat. Do it now or you'll be sorry!'

Sara felt for the old upturned boat and sat down on it. It was dark, but she could just see the thin **figure** of a man next to her. He was holding a flashlight. He turned it on and shone the bright light into her face. Sara saw that he was wearing dark clothes. A black **hood** was over his hair and most of his face. He moved angrily, but Sara could see that he was nervous, too.

figure someone that you can't see very well

hood something that you wear over your head

'Where's the money?' asked the man. 'Did you bring it?'

'Where's Luke?' asked Sara.

The man laughed. 'First things first. Give me the money and then you can see your boyfriend.'

'It's in the bag over there,' said Sara. 'Get it yourself.'

The man looked around for the bag, which was on the floor. For a minute, he was not looking at Sara. Now was the time to do something, she thought. Quickly, she took the taser from her pocket and turned it on the man. There was a noise from the taser. With a loud cry, he fell to the ground. He was **conscious**, but he couldn't move.

Sara took out her flashlight and shone it at his head. She then took the black hood in her hand and quickly pulled it off. There in front of her was the face of the thin, dark man from the photo on Gina's computer. It was the same face that she saw reflected in the window at the mall when she was with Luke. Her suspicions were right.

Sara shouted, 'Tell me where Luke is or I'll hurt you again! I'm serious. Tell me!' She held the taser near his body.

The man cried out, 'No, don't hurt me! Look! He's here!'

'Don't be stupid!' shouted Sara. 'There's no other person here. Tell me where he is, now!'

'He's under the boat!' he cried. 'It's true! See for yourself!'

The old boat was heavier than it looked and Sara hurt her hands trying to move it. She tried a few times until she finally pulled it up and put it against the wall. Luke lay there in a ball under the boat. She cried out when she saw him. His clothes were dirty and his shirt had blood all over it. There were cuts on his face and he wasn't wearing any shoes. Worst of all, he wasn't moving. Sara shouted loudly, 'Luke, Luke! Are you OK? Answer me!' But there was no reply.

Sara screamed at the man on the floor, 'What have you done to him? You've killed him!'

'No, I haven't!' the man **gasped**. 'He isn't dead. Look, you

conscious
awake and knowing what is happening around you

gasp to take a short, quick breath because you are surprised

are free to go. Just leave me the money and get out. Your boyfriend will wake up soon. I'm not alone, you know. I have friends near here. They're coming to help me and they aren't very nice people.'

'None of that is true!' Sara shouted. 'I'm not leaving without him and you are going to leave with the police.' Sara touched Luke's face and spoke to him again. 'Hold on, Luke. Help will be here soon.' She took out her phone and called Sandy.

'Sandy, I'm sorry to wake you,' she said quickly. 'I'm in Clark's boathouse down by the river. Send a police car. I know how Gina died and I have her killer here. We need an ambulance, too. Luke is here. He's badly hurt'. Her voice broke. 'And I don't know if he's going to live.'

'It's OK, Sara,' said Sandy. 'Help is coming right now. Everything will be all right.'

The man on the floor was beginning to move his arms and legs again. Slowly, he started to move towards the door. But Sara was very worried about Luke and she didn't see what was happening. When she looked up, it was too late. The door of the boathouse was open and the man was gone.

READING CHECK

Are these sentences true or false? Tick the boxes.

		True	False
a	Sara finds out that Gina was asking someone for money.	☑	☐
b	She recognizes the man on Gina's computer.	☐	☐
c	She works well at school that day.	☐	☐
d	She doesn't tell her father that she is going to the boathouse again.	☐	☐
e	She puts $50,000 into a bag.	☐	☐
f	She takes her father's taser without telling him.	☐	☐
g	Cody kills Sara when she arrives at the boathouse.	☐	☐
h	Sara sits down on the upturned boat.	☐	☐
i	Sara finds Luke under the old boat.	☐	☐
j	Cody escapes from the boathouse when Sara is with Luke.	☐	☐

WORD WORK

1 Find words or phrases from Chapter 6

cjitaserposl

quhoodly

aspuconsciouser

dijfileg

ijfigureop

lkopigasp

2 Choose the correct word from Activity 1 to complete the sentences.

a I didn't recognize the man because he was wearing a *file* / *hood* on his head.

b When he saw all the blood on the floor he gave a loud *hood* / *gasp*.

c I can see the *figure* / *gasp* of a person through the trees but I don't know who it is.

d A *gasp* / *taser* can't kill someone but it is still dangerous.

e I keep all my work in a special *file* / *hood* on my computer.

f The man is *file* / *conscious*, but he is badly hurt and he can't talk.

GUESS WHAT

What do you think these people do in the next chapter? Tick two boxes to finish each sentence.

a Cody …

1 ☐ escapes and jumps into the water.

2 ☐ can't swim across the river.

3 ☐ dies at the hands of Luke.

b Sara …

1 ☐ runs after Cody.

2 ☐ stays in the boathouse with Luke.

3 ☐ phones Sandy.

c Luke …

1 ☐ stays in the boathouse.

2 ☐ is unconscious and can't help Sara.

3 ☐ dies at the hands of Cody.

d Sandy …

1 ☐ catches Cody.

2 ☐ helps Sara.

3 ☐ does not come.

CHAPTER SEVEN
SANDY

Sara ran out of the boathouse holding the taser, leaving Luke behind. She looked into the dark night and shouted, 'You can't escape! The police are coming!' Just then, she heard something heavy fall into the water. She ran towards the river and shone her flashlight. The man's shoes and coat were lying on the grass. He was trying to escape by swimming away, but he wasn't a strong swimmer, and his arms and legs were still **weak** from the taser. The river was fast and cold, and he knew that he could never swim to the other side. He turned onto his back and swam once again to where Sara was waiting. Slowly, he climbed out of the water. He gasped loudly, then fell onto the grass near Sara's feet. Sara wanted to go back to Luke in the boathouse, but she decided to wait until the police arrived. This man must not escape again.

Luckily, she did not have to wait long. Minutes later, two police cars and an ambulance arrived noisily at the scene. Their bright lights shone on and off in the dark. Sandy jumped out of one of the cars and ran up to Sara. Just then, he saw the thin figure in

weak not strong

wet clothes lying twisted on the ground. The man was holding his shaking wet body and talking angrily. Sara was standing over him, the taser in her hand. When she saw Sandy, she suddenly felt very tired. The taser dropped from her hand and fell onto the ground.

'Are you all right, Sara?' asked Sandy. 'What happened?'

Sara spoke shakily. 'This is the man who killed Gina and he **kidnapped** Luke, too. I don't know everything yet because poor Luke is unconscious. He's in the boathouse. This man left him under the old boat to die. We need to take Luke to hospital at once. He's very bad.'

Sandy looked at the man lying near Sara's feet.

'I know this person,' he said. 'It's Cody Wilson. This isn't the first time he's been in trouble, but he's never killed anyone before.'

Sandy moved nearer to the man. 'What have you done now, Cody?' he asked angrily. 'Come on, you can tell me all about it in the car. Remember, if that young man dies, you'll have two murders to your name.'

kidnap to carry someone away when they don't want to go

'But I'm not a murderer,' said Cody. 'I only pushed the stupid girl, and she fell in front of the car. It was an accident. I didn't mean to kill her. And Luke is a friend of mine.'

'What?' laughed Sandy. 'Do you always kidnap your friends, hit them, and leave them under old boats to die?'

'He **owes** me a lot of money,' answered Cody. 'I just wanted to **frighten** him and his girlfriend.'

'All right, let's go,' said Sandy. 'You can explain everything later. Come on, you can stand up now.'

'I can't. It's all her **fault**. She hurt me with that taser thing,' said Cody, looking angrily at Sara. 'And I nearly died in the river.'

'Nobody threw you into the river, Cody. You jumped,' said Sara. Then Sandy took hold of the man and pulled him to his feet. He pushed him towards one of the waiting police cars.

Luke was still unconscious. They carried him into the ambulance. Sara climbed in too, and sat beside him. Sandy put his head round the door just before they left.

'Call your dad, Sara,' he said. 'I've told him that you're fine, but I think he needs to hear it from you.'

'I will, Sandy,' said Sara. 'Thanks for everything.'

Ten minutes later, the ambulance was nearly at the hospital and Luke opened his eyes for the first time.

'Hey, Sara,' he **whispered**. He tried to smile but he was too weak.

'You're awake! How are you feeling?' she said.

'OK, but I'm thirsty. Can I have some water?' he asked.

'I'm really sorry,' she answered. 'I can't give you any water because you have a head injury.'

'Did the police catch Cody?' he said.

Sara smiled. 'No, they didn't. I caught him, but I'll tell you all about it later. Don't talk now.'

'I'm sorry, Sara,' he whispered. 'This is all my fault. I put you in danger.'

owe to have to give back money some time that you have borrowed

frighten to make someone feel afraid or scared

fault when something is your fault, you have done something wrong

whisper to speak very quietly

'Yes, you did. But I'm sure that you had your reasons,' she smiled. 'I have some questions for you, but they can wait until you're better.'

In a few minutes, the ambulance arrived at the hospital. It stopped in front of the big glass doors, which opened immediately. Sara climbed down and stood watching as they took Luke inside the building. She suddenly felt very tired and shaky.

'Are you all right?' one of the medics asked. 'You don't look so good. You're very pale. Can I have a look at your hands?'

Sara looked down in surprise. There were cuts and blood on her hands from moving the boat.

'I'm fine,' she said, 'I just need to call my dad.' She took out her phone.

'Hi, Dad. I'm very sorry about all this,' she began.

'Are you hurt, Sara?' he asked. 'Just tell me that first.'

'No, I'm not,' she said. 'Luke is conscious now so he's going to be all right, too. I'm sorry that I didn't tell you everything, Dad. It was truly wrong to take your taser, I can see that now.'

'You did WHAT?' he shouted. 'I didn't know! Never do anything like that again, Sara, please. Come home at once and tell me all about it.'

'I'll be there very soon, Dad,' said Sara. 'I just need to speak to the doctors first about Luke.'

READING CHECK

Who says these things? Match the words with the people and the situations.

1 'You can't escape!'

2 'The water's too cold!'

3 'Never do anything like this again.'

4 'Can I have some water?'

5 'Phone your dad, Sara.'

6 'Let me see your hands.'

a Luke asks Sara in the ambulance.

b Sandy tells Sara when Cody is in the police car.

c The medic says to Sara outside the hospital.

d Cody says to himself when he tries to swim away.

e Mr. Dixon says to Sara when he learns about the taser.

f Sara says to Cody when he jumps in the river.

WORD WORK

1 Match the pictures with the words.

| frighten   kidnap   owe   fault |

a ....

b ....

c ....

d ....

2 Use words from Activity 1 to correct the boxed words in these sentences.

a I don't like horror movies. They `forget` ...*frighten*...me.

b How much money do you `open` .... to the bank?

c It's the car's `fat` .... that we arrived late. It goes so slowly on the hills!

d That man is very rich and bad people have often tried to `kitchen` .... his children.

GUESS WHAT

What do you think happens in the next chapter? Tick three boxes.

a ☐ Luke comes out of the hospital.

b ☐ Luke and Sara say goodbye forever.

c ☐ Sara and her dad cook for their friends.

d ☐ Carlie and Luke marry.

e ☐ Luke explains what happened with Cody.

f ☐ Sara decides to be a teacher and forget about detective work.

Chapter Eight
OLD FRIENDS

Two weeks after the scene at the boathouse, Luke came out of hospital and went home. He had some small cuts on his face and two of his front teeth were **missing**, but he felt much better. When he went into his apartment, his eyes immediately fell on a note lying on the table. It was from Sara.

Hi Luke,
Welcome home! There's food in the house for you. But if you prefer, you can come and have supper with Dad and me. Sandy is coming too and he really wants to see you.
I hope you can come.
Sara x

Luke smiled. Good food and friends were just what he needed. He called Sara.

'Hey, it's me. Thanks for buying the food. I'd love to see you all tonight. What time shall I come? About seven o'clock? Fine. Can I bring anything? OK, I'll see you later.'

At 7.30, Luke was resting on the sofa at Sara's house. She was in the kitchen with her father. They were making supper together. Both of them enjoyed cooking and now they had the **chance** to talk, too.

'I think that your spaghetti will be great for Luke, Dad', said Sara. 'He can't eat very well since Cody knocked out his teeth.'

Mr. Dixon's face went dark and he began to look very serious.

'Poor Luke. Cody nearly killed him,' he whispered. 'I hope that he goes to prison for a long time.'

missing not there

welcome we say this when when we want to be friendly to someone

chance the possibility that something can happen

'He will, Dad, don't worry. Gina died because of him and Luke was badly hurt. Cody's **guilty** of more than just robbery, kidnapping, and blackmail,' explained Sara.

'Well, Gina was unlucky,' he said. 'She tried to blackmail Cody after he robbed her and that was a big mistake. She wasn't the best person in the world, but she paid with her life, poor girl'.

'Yes, Cody's a dangerous man,' said Sara. 'He hit her too hard and she fell into the street. He probably wanted to frighten her, not kill her. That was when Luke saw him and decided to go and confront him. That's why he left me so suddenly in the street.'

'I never really understood how he knew Cody in the first place,' said Mr. Dixon. 'What was the connection between the two of them?'

Before Sara could reply, the doorbell rang and she went to answer it.

Carlie was standing in the street, smiling, and holding out a box of chocolates.

'Oh, welcome, good you came!' cried Sara. 'Luke's here already. He'll be happy to see you.'

Just then, Sandy arrived too. 'I hope I'm not late!' he said.

guilty when you have done something wrong or bad

49

Sara and her dad sat at one side of the table and Sandy and Carlie were at the other side. Luke sat at the top of the table and smiled round at the happy group.

'Wow,' he said. 'This is great. A room filled with all my favorite people.'

They finished their spaghetti and Sara brought in some cheese and fruit.

'There's some soft cheese for you, Luke,' she said. 'It'll be easier to eat.'

Luke drank some water, put down his glass, and looked around the table at his friends.

'I never explained fully about Cody,' he said. 'We weren't friends, but he lived in the same street as me when I was a boy. He was always in trouble at school but for some reason he followed me around all the time.

'After he left school, he got a job in a garage and I didn't see him again for a while. Then we met by accident in a café. He looked rich to me. He had good clothes and a very nice car. People said he was making money **illegally**, so I stayed away from him. But then things started to go wrong for my company. I owed money to people who were working for me and I had no money to grow the business.

'One afternoon, I was feeling very bad and I met Cody in the street. We went for a coffee and I told him my problems. He said that he had lots of cash. I could borrow some and pay him back in a few months. I was weak and I took the money. But I couldn't pay it back quickly and Cody started to **threaten** me. The money that I owed him grew and grew. I had to tell someone, so I talked to Carlie. I didn't tell her Cody's name, but she knew that someone was blackmailing me. I'm sorry, Carlie. It was my fault that things were difficult between you and Sara. I didn't want to tell Sara because she always wants to help and it was too dangerous.'

'Yes, that's true,' Carlie said. She turned to Sara. 'I was telling

illegal not legal; you can go to prison for doing something illegal

threaten to say that you will do something bad to someone to make them feel afraid

you the truth, Sara. I really didn't know much about it.'

'And you weren't going out with Luke?' asked Sara, smiling.

'Of course not!' Carlie said.

Sandy was the next person to speak.

'Luke, tell me this. Why did you run after Cody when the accident happened?' he asked.

'I knew he was in town because I saw him behind me in the mall. He was trying to frighten me and he was doing a good job! Then I saw him again at the scene of the accident and I was sure that he had something to do with that, too. I wanted him

to stop blackmailing me, so I decided to confront him. Of course, he became very angry. He pushed me into an empty old house and we fought. He's a better fighter than me and he knocked me unconscious. Later, he took me to the boathouse and hid me under the boat. Luckily, Sara came and found me. I was a dead man until then. Cody had to keep me prisoner – he didn't want people to know about his crimes.'

'I'm guessing, Sara, that you made investigations into Gina too,' said Sandy. 'That phone call about the robbery left me suspicious.'

'Er, yes,' Sara said. 'I'm afraid I went into Gina's room. It was easy to get into her computer and I found some interesting email messages from Gina to Cody. I knew about the robbery in her room. Gina saw a chance to make some money from the robber. Cody took Gina's phone, but every time he used it, Gina knew about it through her computer. Cody took photos of himself and Gina used them to find out all about him. Then she started to blackmail him and threaten him with the police. Cody decided to teach her a lesson. But it all went too far and Gina died.'

Silence fell in the room. After a minute, Mr. Dixon took his glass in his hand and turned to look at his daughter. 'Let's drink to Sara, and everything she's done. And let's hope that she never has to do it again!'

'To Sara,' everyone said together.

READING CHECK

Correct the mistakes in the sentences.

a When Luke goes into his apartment he sees a note from ~~Cody~~ *Sara*.

b Sara and her dad cook breakfast for everybody.

c Mr. Dixon is happy that Cody put Luke's life in danger.

d Luke can't eat easily because he has lost some of his hair.

e Luke knew Cody at work when he was a boy.

f Luke borrowed cars from Cody.

g Carlie knew a lot about Luke and Cody.

h Cody pushed Gina and she fell into the river.

i Cody knew that Sara's family was quite poor.

j Luke is happy that he put Sara in danger.

WORD WORK

Use the words below to complete the sentences. The words are used more than once.

> illegal   threaten   welcome

a It's . . . . to drive on the right in England.

b You can . . . . me, but I won't tell you the secret.

c You are . . . . to come to the party tomorrow night.

d . . . . back! You've been away for a long time!

e Is smoking . . . . in restaurants in this country?

f . . . . to call the police. He'll leave us alone if you do that.

GUESS WHAT

What happens after the story ends? Choose from these ideas or add your own.

a ☐ Sara starts to go out with Carlie.

b ☐ Mr. Dixon marries again and Sara leaves home.

c ☐ Luke's company grows and he is very happy.

d ☐ Sara passes her exams and goes to university.

e ☐ ....
....

f ☐ ....
....

Project A · *Young detectives*

**1 Read the text and write notes in the information table below. Use a dictionary to
help you.**

Theodore Boone

Theodore Boone is a young boy detective created by
John Grisham, a well-known crime writer from the USA.
Grisham was a lawyer before he became a writer, so he
knows a lot about the law and how it works.

There are several books where Theodore, usually called
Theo, is the main character. In the first book, published
in 2010, Theo is thirteen and is still in school. He is an
only child. Both of his parents are lawyers and they work
together in the same office. Theo spends a lot of time
there and he finds his parents' work very interesting. He

John Grisham

often helps to investigate crimes and sometimes he goes to court as a witness. In fact, the
courtroom is one of his favorite places, and he finds it much more interesting than school.
Theo is a clever boy and he can speak well in court, but in many ways he is just like other
teenage boys. He has a bike, and he and his friends spend a lot of time riding around
the town. His friends often help him to solve crimes. Another of Theo's helpers is his dog,
Judge. Judge spends part of his time at home and the rest of his time at the office. He is a
clever animal and sometimes rescues Theo when he is in trouble.

Name of detective	Theodore Boone
Creator	
From	
Year of first book	
Age	
Family	
He is good at	
He gets help from	
Other information	

2 **Read the notes about another famous young detective and complete the text below.**

Name of detective	Nancy Drew
Creator	Edward Stratemeyer
From	USA
Year of first book	1930
Age	Eighteen
Family	only child, lives with father, a lawyer
She is good at	sports
She gets help from	her two cousins
Other information	she drives a hybrid car; she has appeared in computer games; a number of different people have written about her.

. . . . .is a girl detective in a mystery fiction series. She was created in . . . . .by a publisher called Edward Stratemeyer, and she first appeared in a book in . . . . Since then hundreds of books have been written about her. They are sold all over the world in many languages. A number of . . . . .have written about Nancy and her adventures. Most of them do not write under their real names. Over the years, Nancy's changed a lot!

In 2004 the original Nancy Drew mystery stories came to an end and a new series started called *Girl Detective*. In 2013, *Girl Detective* also finished and another series started called *The Nancy Drew Diaries*.

In these latest books, Nancy Drew is about . . . . .years old. She is a girl of action and she is very good at . . . . She drives a hybrid . . . . .and uses a cell phone. Nancy lives with her father, a . . . ., in the town of River Heights. She often solves her mysteries with the help of her two . . . ., Bess and George.

Nancy is popular all over the world. She has appeared in five movies, two television shows, and a number of popular . . . .

3 **Do you know about any other young detectives in books or movies? Research and write about one of them, using the texts in Activities 1 and 2 to help you.**

Project B *Interviewing a character*

1 Complete the interview with Mr. Dixon. Put the questions in the correct place. Use a dictionary to help you.

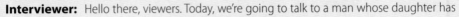

> Don't you ever worry about her getting hurt?
>
> Did you take her to the laboratory to show her what you do?
>
> ~~When did you first realize that Sara was different?~~
>
> Do you think that your work with the police had a strong influence on her?
>
> Does she want to work with the police when she's older, or does she have other plans?

Interviewer: Hello there, viewers. Today, we're going to talk to a man whose daughter has become very famous over the past few weeks. Of course, I'm talking about John Dixon, father of Sara Dixon, Young Detective of the Year. Welcome to the programme, Mr. Dixon. You must be very proud of your daughter.

Mr. Dixon: Yes, I am, thank you.

Interviewer: **a)** When did you first realize that Sara was different?

Mr. Dixon: Well, I don't think she is different. She just enjoys finding things out more than other people!

Interviewer: **b)** ....

Mr. Dixon: Oh, yes, definitely. She always loved hearing about my job. She never stopped asking questions.

Interviewer: **c)** ....

Mr. Dixon: Well, we can't take young children to the lab, It's against the law. However, she always had a very good idea of what I do. We talked about it a lot.

Interviewer: She did very well in catching Cody, a very violent man. **d)** ....

Mr. Dixon: Of course I do. I'm proud of her, but I don't want her to do anything like this again. It's much too dangerous.

Interviewer: **e)** ....

Mr. Dixon: At the moment, police work is definitely at the top of her list. But she's only seventeen. Things can change a lot in a few years.

Interviewer: Yes, indeed. Thank you, Mr. Dixon. And please give my congratulations to Sara.

Mr. Dixon: I'll do that. Thank you very much.

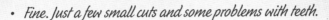

2 **Complete the interview with Luke. Write answers to the interviewer's questions using the notes.**

- Fine. Just a few small cuts and some problems with teeth.

- No, wanted to go, but had to go to the dentist! (why?)

- Fantastic. A great girl. Very proud of her.

- Yes. The company is growing. Sara and her dad helped. (how?)

- To go on working hard. Also to take a vacation very soon. (where?)

- No. We have a lot of things to do before that.

Interviewer: Yesterday, we talked to John Dixon, father of Sara, our Young Detective of the Year. Today, we are talking to her boyfriend, Luke. Hi, Luke. Welcome to the programme. First of all, how are you feeling after everything that's happened to you?

Luke: ....

Interviewer: I'm happy to hear it. Did you go with Sara to the big party for Young Detective of the Year?

Luke: ....

Interviewer: What do you think of her actions?

Luke: ....

Interviewer: She saved your life and I believe she also saved your company. Is that right?

Luke: ....

Interviewer: What are your plans for the future?

Luke: ....

Interviewer: Are you and Sara getting married any time soon?

Luke: ....

3 Prepare questions for an interview with Sandy or Sara.

4 Imagine that you are Sandy or Sara. Prepare answers to the questions in Activity 3.

5 Work in pairs. Roleplay the interview with a partner.

GRAMMAR CHECK

Tag endings with different tenses

We use question tags to check information, or to ask someone to agree with us. The tag contains a main verb or an auxiliary verb + a subject to match the sentence. When the sentence is affirmative, the question tag is negative. When the sentence is negative, the question tag is affirmative.

You can swim, can't you?   *You can't swim, can you?*

With most tenses, we repeat the main verb or auxiliary verb in the question tag.

She isn't a murderer, is she?   *He was afraid, wasn't he?*

Luke hasn't called, has he?   *We won't lose our money, will we?*

With affirmative Present Simple or Past Simple verbs, we use do or did in the question tag.

You work with him, don't you?   *I sold the car quickly, didn't I?*

1 **What did Sara say to Luke? Complete the questions with tag endings.**

a You aren't tired, *are you* ....?

b You don't need more money, ...?

c You'll have a great company, ...?

d You have your phone, ...?

e You don't need to buy anything, ...?

2 **What did Luke say to Sara? Use the prompts to make sentences.**

a You / need me
   ...*You need me, don't you?*...

b The company / not doing / well

   ....

c Your dad / be / rich

   ....

d We / be going / to the mall

   ....

e My computers / not be / very good

   ....

GRAMMAR CHECK

Adjectives ending in *-ing* and *-ed*

We use adjectives ending in -ing to talk about things, events, and people that make us feel different things.

Sandy had an exciting job

Gina's death was very shocking.

We use adjectives ending in -ed to talk about how people feel.

Luke was excited when he started his company.

Sara was shocked by Gina's death.

3 **Choose the correct words to complete the sentences.**

a When Sara saw that Luke was in a bad mood, she was not *surprised / surprising*.

b Mr. Dixon found his job very *interesting / interested*.

c When Luke saw Cody at the mall, he was *worried / worrying*.

d The thought that Luke was blackmailing her was very *frightened / frightening* to Sara.

e For Sara, being with Luke was sometimes *bored / boring*.

f At first, Luke found his work very *exciting / excited*.

g Sara never felt *boring / bored* when she was investigating something.

h Luke was usually *interested / interesting* in Sara's life.

i Sara felt *frightened / frightening* when Cody pushed her.

j The text messages on Sara's phone were *surprised / surprising*.

k The jacket with blood on it was very *worried / worrying*.

l Sara was very *excited / exciting* when she did well on her exams.

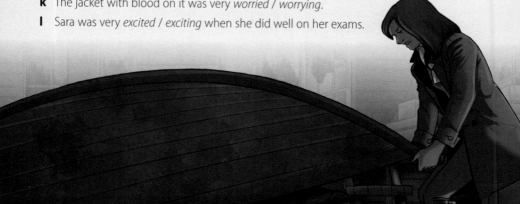

GRAMMAR CHECK

Direct speech and reported speech

In direct speech, we give the words that people say or think. In reported speech, we use a reporting verb (say, tell, ask, think, etc.) and we put the verb in direct speech one step back into the past. We also change the pronouns (I, you, etc.) and the possessive adjectives (my, our, etc.) We usually use that to introduce reported statements.

'I'm going to hurt Sara,' thought Luke.   *Luke thought that he was going to hurt Sara.*

'I can't tell my father about Luke,' said Sara.   *Sara said that she couldn't tell her father about Luke.*

When we report questions with the verb be, we change the order of the subject and verb. We use a question word (what, where, when, etc.) instead of that to introduce a reported information question.

'What are you thinking, Carlie?' asked Sara. (= verb + subject)

Sara asked Carlie what she was thinking. (= subject + verb)

4 Write the sentences as reported speech.

a 'We need some new computers,' Luke explained.

..Luke explained that they needed some new computers.....

b 'Rich people don't understand anything', he said.

c 'What are you doing, Sara?' Sandy asked.

d 'I know a lot of students,' Sara said.

e 'Gina is blackmailing someone,' thought Sara.

f 'Where are you going, Sara?' Mr. Dixon asked.

g 'The police are coming!' Sara shouted.

h 'I understand, Luke,' said Sandy.

GRAMMAR CHECK

To + infinitive or *-ing* form of verb

After the verbs begin, enjoy, finish, go, go on, like, love, prefer, remember, and stop, we use verb + -ing.

Mr. Dixon prefers working in a laboratory to working in an office.

After the verbs begin, decide, forget, learn, like, need, remember, try, want, and would like, we use to + infinitive.

Sara decided to investigate Gina's death.

With the verb remember, the meaning changes with to + infinitive or verb + -ing.

Sara remembered to take a flashlight with her to the boathouse.

(= the remembering is first and looks forward to taking the flashlight)

Sara remembered seeing Cody in the mall.

(= the remembering is second and looks back to the time at the mall)

With the verbs begin and like, the meaning does not change.

Sara likes to shop / shopping on Saturday mornings.

Luke began to work / working when he was twenty-two.

5 **Complete the sentences about the story with the *to* + infinitive or verb + *-ing* form of the verb in brackets. Use a dictionary to help you.**

a Sara would like .. to have .... (have) a job like her father's.

b Luke didn't really want .... (go) to the mall.

c Sara was worried, but she went on .... (talk) to Luke.

d After the accident, Sara tried .... (help) the police.

e She remembered .... (see) Gina before at her school.

f Sara usually enjoyed .... (work) with the police.

g She remembered .... (take) the key to Luke's apartment.

h When he finished .... (watch) the news, Mr. Dixon went to bed.

i Sara needed .... (find out) more about Cody.

j On the path to the river, she began .... (feel) afraid.

k On her second visit to the boathouse, Sara didn't forget .... (wear) warm clothes.

l Luke enjoyed .... (eat) supper with all his friends.

GRAMMAR

GRAMMAR CHECK

Modal auxiliary verbs: *can*, *could*, *must*, and *have to*

We use can (can't) / could (not) + infinitive without *to* to express requests, permission, or ability.   *Can / Could I ask you about something? (= request)*

You can cross the street when the light is green. (= permission)

She can run very fast. (= general ability)

Sara couldn't find her flashlight. (= past ability)

We use must (not) + infinitive without *to* for strong obligation or prohibition.

I must find Luke quickly. (=strong obligation)

You mustn't drive on the right in England. (= prohibition)

We use have to / don't have to + infinitive without *to* when something is necessary / not necessary.   *I have to go.*

There is a big difference in meaning between don't have to and mustn't.

You don't have to do that. (= it is not necessary)   You mustn't do that. (= it is not a good idea)

I have to go to school. (= obligation from outside the speaker)

We use had to for obligation in the past.   *She had to leave.*

---

6 **Choose the correct modal verb in the sentences.**

   a Sara wanted to tell her father about Luke but she ~~couldn't~~ / can't.

   b '*Could / Have* you cook supper tonight?' asked Mr. Dixon.

   c Cody said, 'You *must / have* be very careful, Sara.'

   d Sara *had / could* to find out what Luke was doing.

   e 'I *can / have* to look in Gina's room', said Sandy.

7 **Complete the text with suitable modal forms.**

Sara **a)** ..couldn't.......... ask Luke too many questions because he was in a bad mood. But

she **b)** .... find out why he was so unhappy.

After the accident, Sara **c)** .... help Sandy with his questions about Gina.

After that, she tried to talk to Luke but she **d)** .... because he wasn't

answering his phone. 'I **e)** .... find out why he ran away,' she thought.

That night, Sara asked **f)** '.......................... we watch the news? I want to hear about Gina.'

Mr. Dixon **g)** .... go to bed early because he was tired. Sara went to the

boathouse, but nobody came. 'I **h)** .... phone Carlie', she thought. 'She'll

know what to do.' But Carlie **i)** .... tell Sara very much about Luke.

GRAMMAR CHECK

Past Simple and Past Continuous

We use the Past Simple for finished past events. We us the Past Continuous for an activity that was in progress when events in the Past Simple happened. We use was / were + present participle to make the Past Continuous. We often use when to introduce the Past Simple verb and while to introduce the Past Continuous verb.

Luke and Sara were waiting to cross the street when the accident happened.

The accident happened while Luke and Sara were waiting to cross the street.

With stative verbs – for example, feel, love, like, think, and want – we don't usually use the Past Continuous.

Mr. Dixon ~~was liking his job~~.   *Mr. Dixon liked his job.* ✔

---

8 Answer the questions about the beginning of the story. Use the words in brackets.

a What was Sara doing at home on Saturday morning? (wait / in her room / Luke)

....She was waiting in her room for Luke............................

b What was Mr. Dixon doing? (get ready / go to work)

....

c How did Luke feel? (feel / bad)

....

d What did Luke do while he was walking around the mall? (think / troubles)

....

e What were the people in the mall doing? (buying things / stores)

....

9 Put the verbs in brackets in the text into the Past Simple or the Past Continuous.

While Luke **a)** ..was walking..... (walk) around the mall, he **b)** ....
(see) Cody behind him. He **c)** .... (stare) at Luke in the store window.
Luke and Sara **d)** .... (go) to have something to eat, but while he
e) .... (eat), Luke was in a bad mood and he didn't talk much. They left
the mall and went out into the street. While they **f)** .... (wait) on the
sidewalk, something terrible **g)** .... (happen). They suddenly
h) .... (hear) a loud noise and when they looked across the street,
they saw a young girl. She **i)** .... (lie) in the street and she
j) .... (not move). While someone **k)** .... (call)
the police, Sara **l)** .... (run) across the street to see if she could help.

GRAMMAR CHECK

Reflexive pronouns

We use reflexive pronouns (myself, yourself, himself, herself, itself, ourselves, yourselves, and themselves) when the subject and the object of the verb are the same.

She sometimes asked herself about Luke's feelings.

The cat hurt itself in the accident.

The students told themselves that the exam was easy.

We can also use reflexive pronouns to emphasize who did something, or for things that a person does alone without anybody else.

Luke ate very little himself.   *Sara found the answer herself.*

10 Read Sara's diary. Complete the text with the words in the box.

> himself   ~~myself~~   itself   ourselves   themselves   himself
> himself   herself   itself   myself

I sometimes ask **a)** ...myself.... if Luke really loves me. I'm worried about him. The other day, he was talking to **b)** .... in the car. Something is making him nervous. The company **c)** .... is not doing well. I think Luke needs more money. I talked to Carlie about it, but she didn't tell me much. I tell **d)** .... that there is nothing between Carlie and Luke, but I can't be sure. She told me **e)** .... that they are just friends. She's my best friend and I want to believe her.

School is difficult too these days, since Gina died. All the students are asking **f)** .... what really happened to her. The accident **g)** .... is a mystery. Did someone push Gina?

Dad says that we have to look after **h)** .... and not worry too much. I suppose that he's right. He doesn't always look after **i)** ...., I must say. I think he works too hard. He does too much **j)** .... I think that he needs more help at work.

DOMINOES Your Choice

Read *Dominoes* for pleasure, or to develop language skills. It's your choice.

Each *Domino* reader includes:
- a good story to enjoy
- integrated activities to develop reading skills and increase vocabulary
- task-based projects – perfect for CEFR portfolios
- contextualized grammar activities

Each *Domino* pack contains a reader, and an excitingly dramatized audio recording of the story

If you liked this *Domino*, read these:

Who am I?
Or, the Modern Frankenstein
Emma Howell

Vic has no friends. Everyone else has friends, and it makes him angry. So, Vic makes a new name for himself online, so he can make other people feel the way he does. But soon Vic finds it difficult to control what he has created…

Will Vic's mistake hurt people, or can he stop it in time? What will happen to Vic? And what will happen to the monster he has made?

Jemma's Jungle Adventure
Anne Collins

Jemma is very excited when she joins an expedition to the island of Kamora. She hopes to learn about doing scientific research, and to find a very rare bird of paradise.

She is happy to meet the famous Dr Malone and the wise Dr Al Barwani, and to help to research birds, snakes, and insects. But things start to go wrong. Someone has a terrible secret, and there is danger for Jemma – and for the bird.

Who has a secret plan, and what is it? What will happen to the bird? And what will happen to Jemma?

	CEFR	Cambridge Exams	IELTS	TOEFL iBT	TOEIC
Level 3	B1	PET	4.0	57-86	550
Level 2	A2–B1	KET-PET	3.0-4.0	–	390
Level 1	A1–A2	YLE Flyers/KET	3.0	–	225
Starter & Quick Starter	A1	YLE Movers	1.0–2.0	–	–

You can find details and a full list of books and teachers' resources on our website:
www.oup.com/elt/gradedreaders